Copyright

Author Website: JeVonaManiex.com
Email: GraceGritBooks@gmail.com
All names, events, and experiences described herein reflect the author's true story. In some cases, identifying details have been changed to protect privacy.

Interior Design: Shumaila Khan
Printed in the United States of America

Dedication

For every woman who has ever survived silence.
For every soul who has ever felt unseen,
unheard, or unworthy.
May you know that your story matters, your
healing is holy,
and your voice is proof that resurrection is
possible.

Table of contents

RICH IN GRACE I

COPYRIGHT PAGE II

DEDICATION III

PROLOGUE: HELL IN HEAVEN VII

PART I: THE FOUNDATIONS ••••••••••••••••••••••••• X

TESTIMONY ONE: FOUNDATIONS OF SURVIVAL AND
STRENGTH 01

    Reader's Guide 04

TESTIMONY TWO: THE TOP BUNK 06

    Reader's Guide 07

TESTIMONY THREE: PRAYING FOR AN END 09

    Reader's Guide 10

TESTIMONY FOUR: THE NUMBER 29 13

    Reader's Guide 16

TESTIMONY FIVE: "YOU MUST HAVE LIKED IT" 18

    Reader's Guide 20

TESTIMONY SIX: THE CHOICE 22

    Reader's Guide 24

TESTIMONY SEVEN: POTPIES AND NEW SHOES ... 26

    Reader's Guide 28

PART II: THE GATHERING STORM ••••••••••••••••• 30

TESTIMONY EIGHT: BREATHING ROOM 31

    Reader's Guide 33

Table of contents

TESTIMONY NINE: THREE PAGES IN MICHIGAN 35

Reader's Guide 37

TESTIMONY TEN: CROSSING THRESHOLDS 39

Reader's Guide 41

PART III: THE FIRE ••• **44**

TESTIMONY ELEVEN: THE COST OF OBEDIENCE 45

Reader's Guide 47

TESTIMONY TWELVE: FAITH IN THE FIRE 50

Reader's Guide 51

TESTIMONY THIRTEEN: CHOOSING SANITY 54

Reflection: The Holy Work of Stopping 56

Reader's Guide 57

TESTIMONY FOURTEEN: THE EYES IN THE BACK OF MY MIND 58

Reflection: Living With the Echoes 60

Reader's Guide 61

TESTIMONY FIFTEEN: FELICIA, MY ANCHOR 63

Reflection: The Ministry of Presence 64

Reader's Guide 65

PART IV: THE RESURRECTION ••••••••••••••••••••••••••• **67**

TESTIMONY SIXTEEN: RESTORATION IS A PROCESS 68

Reflection: The Slow Work of God 69

TESTIMONY SEVENTEEN: LOVE, WAR, AND THE MIRROR 72

Reflection: When Love Meets the Mirror 73

Reader's Guide 74

Table of contents

TESTIMONY EIGHTEEN THE MASK AND THE MIRROR ⸺⸺⸺⸺ 76

The Mask and the Mirror — Closing Reflection ⸺⸺⸺ 77
Reader's Guide ⸺⸺⸺⸺⸺⸺⸺⸺⸺⸺⸺ 78

TESTIMONY NINETEEN: THE RESURRECTION OF ME ⸺⸺ 80

Reflection: The Courage to Be Seen ⸺⸺⸺⸺⸺ 81
Reader's Guide ⸺⸺⸺⸺⸺⸺⸺⸺⸺⸺⸺ 82

BRIDGE: FROM MASK TO RESURRECTION ⸺⸺⸺⸺⸺ 84

THE RESURRECTION OF ME — CLOSING REFLECTION ⸺⸺ 84

TESTIMONY TWENTY: A NEW PATTERN ⸺⸺⸺⸺⸺⸺ 85

Reader's Guide ⸺⸺⸺⸺⸺⸺⸺⸺⸺⸺⸺ 86

Epilogue: Unmasked ⸺⸺⸺⸺⸺⸺⸺⸺⸺ 88
Final Prayer for the Reader ⸺⸺⸺⸺⸺⸺⸺ 89
A Benediction ⸺⸺⸺⸺⸺⸺⸺⸺⸺⸺⸺ 89
Acknowledgments ⸺⸺⸺⸺⸺⸺⸺⸺⸺⸺ 90

EPILOGUE: UNMASKED ⸺⸺⸺⸺⸺⸺⸺⸺⸺ 93

Post-Epilogue: Still Rising October 3, 2025 ⸺⸺⸺ 94
Author's Note of Gratitude ⸺⸺⸺⸺⸺⸺⸺ 95
Back Cover Blurb ⸺⸺⸺⸺⸺⸺⸺⸺⸺⸺ 96
About the Author ⸺⸺⸺⸺⸺⸺⸺⸺⸺⸺ 97
Grace & Grit Books ⸺⸺⸺⸺⸺⸺⸺⸺⸺ 98

Prologue: Hell in Heaven

"Healing isn't a destination; it's a rhythm."

This memoir is by no means meant to sadden you, but to encourage you —and to lift or reignite your life light.

I've always believed that healing isn't a destination; it's a rhythm. It ebbs and flows with every breath, decision, prayer, and scar. There are chapters in my life I never would've written for myself—yet they are the ink that gave birth to my becoming.

Hell in Heaven describes the paradox of my life. The very places and people that should have been safe havens often became the sites of my deepest wounds. Family was supposed to be heaven—but at times, it felt like hell. Home was supposed to mean comfort—but it carried the sting of abuse and silence. Even faith communities, workplaces, and friendships sometimes mirrored the same contradiction: promise wrapped in betrayal, and joy shadowed by pain.

This is what makes trauma so sharp—it hides in the places we thought would protect us. And yet, even in those places, God's hand never let me go. What was meant for harm, He has carried through into healing.

So yes, there was hell in my heaven. But there was also heaven in my hell— because the presence of God, even in fire, became my lifeline.

My name is Dr. JeVona Maniex. And this is my story—unfinished, unfolding, but deeply mine.

Reflection

Healing rarely comes in straight lines. It loops, repeats, stumbles, and sometimes dances when you least expect it. I've learned that we don't have to erase the hard chapters to find peace—we just need to reframe them. This book is my rhythm of healing.

May it help you find yours.

> *"Even if my father and mother abandon me, the Lord cares for me."*
> —Psalm 27:10 (CSB)

Reader's Guide

Affirmation

I accept that both pain and beauty have shaped me, and I choose to see God's presence in every season.

 **Prayer:**

God, thank You for never leaving me—even when the places and people I trusted most failed me. Teach me to find Your heaven even in my hell and help me to carry hope through every fire. Amen.

Reflection Questions:

1. Where in your own life did "heaven" feel like "hell"?
2. How did God's presence sustain you even when people failed you?
3. What rhythms of healing are you learning to embrace in your own story?

Your Turn: Notes, Affirmation & Personal Prayer

Use this space to write your own reflections.

My Notes:

_____

_____

_____

_____

My Affirmation:

_____

_____

_____

_____

My Prayer:

_____

_____

_____

_____

Part I: The Foundations

(Innocence, Family, Early Wounds)

Trigger Warning: This section contains references to childhood abuse, neglect, and early trauma. These stories are shared honestly for the purpose of healing and testimony.

Prelude

Every story begins somewhere—often in the quiet spaces between what we are taught and what we feel. My own foundation was built on both love and fracture, a fragile mixture of laughter and fear, of a deep desire to belong in a home that didn't always feel safe.

These early chapters are shared not for pity, but for truth. Because before there can be healing, the wound must first be named.

Testimony One:

Foundations of Survival and Strength

"I was born into trauma, but I was also born with strength."

From my very first breath, survival wasn't a choice; it was the air I breathed. I came into this world on June 2, 1975, in South Bend, Indiana —a city where the atmosphere seemed to carry both hope and hard truth. As the firstborn of my mother, LW, and my father, Cedric Pearson, I was the first heartbeat of two-family legacies that would soon branch in different directions. Their love created me, but their separate paths shaped the battlefield of our home.

This environment taught me to read rooms before I could properly read books. Childhood wasn't painted in soft colors; it was lived in the spaces between slammed doors and unspoken tensions. I didn't know the term for it then, but my body took meticulous notes. I learned the temperature of a room first, then the sound of footsteps on the floorboards, and only then the expressions on the faces. I knew the sharp silence that followed a strained phone call and the faint scent of my mother's vanilla perfume, a signal that she was gathering her strength. I also learned that my father's quick grins could dissolve into huffs without warning, and that approval wasn't spoken—it was measured in the brief, awkward smile that meant I had successfully made myself invisible.

To stay safe, silence became my shield and obedience the currency that bought scraps of peace. This vigilance, born in brokenness, became the very foundation of my strength.

As the oldest, I often learned lessons without a guide, and when my siblings arrived, I began to straddle the line between daughter and caretaker. I was praised for being "mature for my age," but that maturity was just a mask I wore to hide the child who was swallowing her own needs to make room for others. This internal burden was compounded by external wounds. My dark skin, which should have been celebrated as God's chocolate kiss on my complexion, made me a target for bullying within my own community. I questioned my worth before I truly understood beauty, learning the deep ache of not seeing your own reflection accepted in the eyes of others.

School became both an escape and another proving ground. I loved to learn, but the words swam on the page and letters flipped in my head. I didn't have the language for dyslexia or dysgraphia then; I only knew I had to fight a silent war to make my work look effortless. While teachers praised my performance, they never saw the exhaustion behind my smile or the extra hours it took just to keep up. Each of these battles—at home, in the community, and in the classroom—forged a strange and resilient armor around my heart. Despite it all, I kept showing up. I kept shining, even when others tried to dim my light.

My only true refuge was the one I built in the quiet. Faith wasn't about rigid rituals; it was found in prayers whispered into my pillow when no one else could hear. It was humming gospel songs under my blankets and talking to God as if He were right there in the room with me. In my world, Jesus was never distant; He was closer than the pain, louder than the silence, and steadier than the chaos. Looking back, I see His presence as the unseen force that refused to let me be crushed.

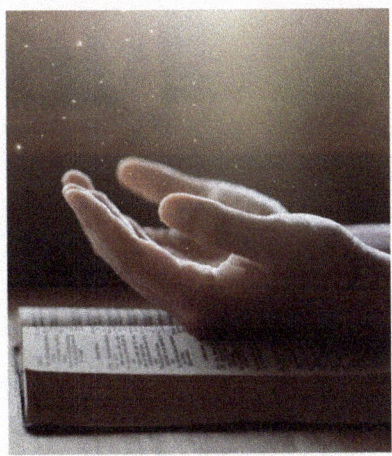

At sixteen, however, that faith faced its greatest test. I was naïve and fumbling with emotions too grown for me to hold, I became pregnant. I thought I was simply being close to a friend, not yet understanding how one act could change a life. Since our fathers were best friends, I clung to the hope that this connection would mean something—that he would stay, that we'd stand together. But he didn't. His rejection was a cut deeper than any I had ever known.

Suddenly, fear consumed me. Other girls spoke of childbirth as a pain so great you could die. I took their terror and my own and laid it before God every single night, begging Him to protect me.

And He did.

On December 20, 1991, I went into labor. In the hospital room, my cousin Felicia, the doctor, the nurses—even my mother—stood in disbelief. I felt no contractions. The nurses had to watch the monitor, not me, and tell my body when to push. Only with the very last push did the pain finally come, but it was fleeting. Then she was here: a five-pound, ten-ounce baby girl, hitting the air with a tiny, angry cry and a grin that Mike Tyson couldn't match.

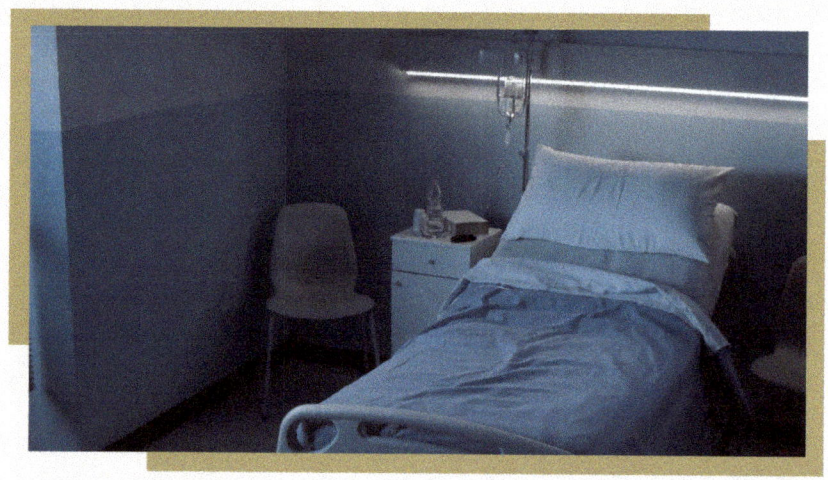

In that moment, I knew. God saw me. He knew my heart, my fear, and my innocence. He had kept me, just as He always had. Holding my daughter, I was determined to give her all the love I was still learning to give myself.

For years, I believed that being "the strong one" was my only option. But holding my daughter, I began to understand that strength doesn't always mean silent endurance. It can look like softness. It can look like asking for help. It can look like finally saying, "I can't carry this alone anymore." That was the beginning of my turning point—the moment I stopped letting my circumstances write my story and started partnering with God to write it myself. As this testimony ends, another begins: the story of healing.

Reflection

We often confuse survival with strength, but true strength begins where survival ends—when we choose healing, ask for help, and speak our truths. I once thought endurance was the only way, but now I know softness is also sacred. This testimony isn't just about what I endured; it's about what I began to reclaim. If you've ever felt unseen, too early grown, or falsely labeled as "the strong one," I see you. You are allowed to be both brave and breaking. Both learning and leading. And you don't have to carry it all alone.

> "God is our refuge and strength, a helper who is always found in times of trouble."
> —Psalm 46:1 (CSB)

Reader's Guide

Affirmation

Even in the hardest beginnings, I carried strength. I am not only what happened to me—I am what God sustained in me.

 **Prayer:**

God, thank you for sustaining me in the shadows. Thank You for being my strength when I was too young to understand Your presence. Help me see that even my survival was a seed of resilience You planted in me. Teach me how to carry forward the strength without carrying forward the pain. Amen.

Reflection Questions:

1. What survival skills did you learn as a child that you still carry today?
2. Which of those skills protected you then, and which do you now need permission to release?
3. How can you honor the strength God placed in you, even through painful seasons?

Your Turn: Notes, Affirmation & Personal Prayer

Use this space to write your own reflections.

My Notes:

_____

_____

_____

_____

My Affirmation:

_____

_____

_____

_____

My Prayer:

_____

_____

_____

_____

Testimony Two:

The Top Bunk

"The safest place in my home was often the place furthest from the ground."

I was eight or nine years old the night life taught me about shame. In the small bedroom I shared with my brother, our bunk bed felt like a coffin in the dark. He slept on the bottom, the safe bunk, close to the floor. I slept on the top. With my mother working the night shift, the house held a different kind of silence—a hollow space where her protection should have been.

That night, it wasn't a sound that pulled me from sleep but a pressure, a weight on my thigh that didn't belong. My eyes fluttered open to the sudden, harsh glare of the ceiling light. He was standing there, his hand on me.

He pulled his hand back quickly. "Oh," he said, his voice straining for a casual tone. "I thought you were Bobby."

The words made no sense. My mind, though sleepy, was instantly, icily clear. How could he think that? He knew my brother slept on the bottom. He knew I was on top. I didn't believe him for a second.

He left, clicking the light off and plunging the room back into darkness. The pressure of his hand was gone, but a new weight had taken its place: the suffocating knowledge that my bed, my room—my own body—was not a safe place. And with Mom gone, there was no one to tell.

In that moment, the top bunk stopped being a perch and became a warning. I learned to sleep lightly, to stay still, to pretend. I learned that even high places weren't beyond reach, and that silence could feel like safety even when it was the furthest thing from it.

Reflection

Looking back, I see how that single night rewrote the map of my body and my trust. It wasn't only the touch; it was the disbelief I anticipated before I could even speak. Trauma isn't just the violation itself but the crushing knowledge that protection may never come. Yet even in that room, on that top bunk, I whispered to God. I didn't have the words for my fear, but He heard me anyway. If you're reading this and remembering your own "top bunk" moment, know this: what happened to you was not your fault, and even in the darkest places, you were never truly unseen..

> **"The Lord is my refuge and my fortress, my God, in whom I trust."**
> **—Psalm 91:2 (CSB)**

Reader's Guide

Affirmation

My body is sacred. My story is sacred. What was violated does not define me. God's protection has always been greater than the harm I endured.

 **Prayer:**

God, You saw me when I felt unseen. You heard the cries I couldn't voice. Thank You for protecting me in ways I may never fully understand. Heal the places where fear still lingers. Restore my trust —first in You, and then, wisely, in others. Amen.

Reflection Questions:

1. What was your "top bunk"—a place that was supposed to be safe but wasn't, or a place you retreated to for safety?
2. How did God's presence carry you in unsafe spaces?
3. What would it mean to reclaim your body and your safety as sacred today?

Your Turn: Notes, Affirmation & Personal Prayer

Use this space to write your own reflections.

My Notes:

_____

_____

_____

_____

My Affirmation:

_____

_____

_____

_____

My Prayer:

_____

_____

_____

_____

Testimony Three:

Praying for an End

> "When the pain became unbearable, I begged God to make it stop."

By the time I was fourteen, the weight of my mother's anger had carved valleys into my spirit. Her voice didn't just correct; it cut. Her hands didn't just discipline; they bruised. Every day in our home felt like walking through a minefield, where I was careful with every step but never truly safe. The smell of dinner cooking could never mask the sharp edge of tension in the air, and my heart would race long before the first angry word was spoken. My body ached in ways no teenager's body should.

One night, the pain became unbearable. It wasn't just the physical sting from another beating that left me reeling in my room; it was the chilling silence that followed. It was the cold dismissal in her eyes when I tried to show her the hurt, the way she looked at me as if I were exaggerating, as if my pain was just a performance. In her gaze, I felt erased.

At fourteen, you don't really want to die; you just want the pain to stop. But when every door to relief seems locked and bolted, death begins to feel like the only key left in your hand. The thought was quiet at first, a whisper in the hollow space left by her rejection. Then it grew louder, promising an end to the shouting, the shame, and the constant, aching loneliness.

So, I decided to walk through that door. I don't need to detail the method; the how is less important than the desperate why.

But in the end I prayed for didn't come. Instead, there was the rough texture of the carpet on my cheek and the confusing, persistent rhythm of my own heartbeat. Lying there, numb and shaking in the aftermath, I whispered a prayer I didn't even know counted as a prayer:

> **"God, please... just let this end."**

And in the stillness of that room, I realized He had. Not by taking my life, but by holding it. My attempt to leave this world became His definitive answer that I was meant to stay. Survival itself was the miracle. Looking back, I see His fingerprints all over the fact that I am still here. The devil intended for that night to be my end, but God marked it as a new beginning. The very moment I thought my story was over, He was already writing the next chapter.

Reflection

I used to think survival was a sign of weakness—that if I couldn't escape the pain, I had failed. Now I know that survival is its own fierce form of strength. At fourteen, I didn't understand why God left me here; today, I understand He left me here because there was more for me to live, to give, and to become. If you've ever begged for an end, please know you're not alone. Sometimes the greatest miracle isn't the pain suddenly stopping, but the simple fact that you're still drawing breath in spite of it.

> *"I will not die, but I will live and proclaim what the Lord has done."*
> *—Psalm 118:17 (CSB)*

Reader's Guide

Affirmation

My survival is not an accident. My life has purpose, and God is still writing my story.

 **Prayer:**

God, thank You for saving me when I didn't want to be saved. Thank You for holding me in the moment I thought my life was over. Teach me to see my survival as evidence of Your love. Remind me that every breath I take is proof that I am not finished. Amen.

Reflection Questions:

- Have you ever prayed for an end and received a different kind of answer?
- What does survival mean to you now compared to what it meant in your past?
- How can you honor the moments when God carried you through what you thought would be the end?

Your Turn: Notes, Affirmation & Personal Prayer

Use this space to write your own reflections.

My Notes:

_____

_____

_____

_____

My Affirmation:

_____

_____

_____

_____

My Prayer:

_____

_____

_____

_____

Testimony Four:

The Number 29

> "Words can wound deeper than fists, and their scars last longer."

There are chapters of my life I never wanted to live—pages I wish I could tear out. But God didn't just let me survive them; He has been rewriting them all along.

I remember one evening at the kitchen table, sitting across from my mother with a stack of flashcards. My little brother leaned against her side as she drilled me over and over on a single card: 29. For me, numbers refused to stay still. Twenty-nine blurred into nineteen; nineteen slipped into ninety-one. Sometimes, 29 would turn itself into 92. Letters flipped, too—an "e" often looked like a "3." The harder I tried to lock them in place, the more they slid away.

My brother must have seen the panic rising in my face because whenever my mother held up the card, he blurted out the right answer before I had a chance to speak, trying to shield me. But instead of relief, his protection only sharpened her anger.

"Are you stupid or something?" she asked. The words pierced deeper than any correction could. Then came the blow that hollowed me out: "Even your little brother knows the number."

Shame landed in my body before it landed in my mind. My throat tightened as my shoulders inched toward my ears. I kept my face still—an old survival skill. In the glow of the table lamp, the number sat there on the flashcard, unblinking and stern. It felt like a stamp of failure, the beginning of a script I never agreed to write. In that moment, it wasn't just a number I struggled with; it was the suffocating shame of being measured and found lacking.

That feeling didn't stay at the kitchen table. It followed me, resurfacing with a particular sting on a cold December morning a few years later when I was eleven. Christmas was supposed to feel magical, but that year, the holiday didn't sparkle; it stung. I sat cross-legged on the floor as my brother and sister unwrapped their gifts.

My infant sister received toys that jingled, and my eight-year-old brother tore through wrapping paper, thrilled with his new trucks.

Then, it was my turn. My mother handed me a small box wrapped in leftover paper. I opened it carefully, hoping for something—anything—that said I mattered. Inside was a can opener. The laughter in the room confirmed it wasn't a mistake but a joke I wasn't in on. "You'll need it one day," she said, her voice sharp with amusement. I didn't laugh. The weight of that gift sent a clear message: You're not a child who dreams; you're a tool to be used. It taught me that love in my home could be practical, but it was rarely personal.

This lesson—that my needs were tasks to be managed, not treasures to be cherished—soon found a new home in my life. By thirteen, that same confusion and shame had wrapped themselves around my own body. For months, my mother would call my father to announce that I had started my period and needed money for pads. But I hadn't, and each premature announcement embarrassed me.

When the day finally came for real, I saw the blood in my underwear and panicked, thinking I was dying. No one had explained what to expect, so I washed myself over and over, trying to make it stop. When my mother eventually noticed and asked, my "yes" led to a silent trip to the drugstore. She bought the supplies with no explanation, no comfort—just another task to check off her list. My first lesson in womanhood came not through guidance, but through secrecy and shame.

These moments—a reversed number, a thoughtless gift, a silent transition into womanhood, a narrative of inadequacy. I didn't have words like dyslexia, dysgraphia, or ADHD to explain why my brain worked differently. All I had were crooked letters and the sting of being corrected without compassion. So, I adapted. I became good at pretending, chasing a kind of perfection that felt like safety. Each certificate I earned later in life became a small act of rebellion against that 29, against that can opener, against every unkind word that told me I wasn't enough.

Years later, when I was finally diagnosed, everything began to make sense. My wiring wasn't broken; it was unique. My brain didn't need fixing; it needed understanding. In that revelation, the shame began to dissolve. God never called me stupid; He called me fearfully and wonderfully made. He knit me together on purpose, with the exact wiring I would one day need to tell my story. This is redemption: how God takes our broken pieces and reshapes them into beauty. He proves that nothing—not a number, not a can opener, not a moment of shame—is ever wasted.

Reflection

Sometimes the deepest scars come not from physical blows but from the quiet, repeated messages that tell a child they're "less than." This chapter is about more than flashcards, gifts, or pads—it's about the silent stories we internalize when no one explains, comforts, or believes. If you've ever been handed a "can opener"

when you were hoping for love, or been measured by a standard you couldn't meet, hear this:

you are not broken. You are not a mistake. And what once marked you with shame can one day become your proof of resilience.

Reader's Guide

Affirmation

Nothing in my story is wasted in the hands of God. My worth was never defined by grades, gifts, or performance. I am not a mistake—I am magnificently designed. I am not a number. I am wonderfully made.

 **Prayer:**

God, thank You for the mind and body You gave me—even when others failed to understand them. Help me hear Your truth louder than the voices that once counted me out. Teach me to celebrate the way You created me, and to extend grace to the younger me who didn't know how to feel safe in her own skin. Amen.

Reflection Questions:

1. What memories shaped how you saw your worth as a child?
2. Which experiences taught you shame—and how can you reclaim those moments now?
3. What does it mean to see yourself as "wonderfully made" even after years of feeling unseen?

Your Turn: Notes, Affirmation & Personal Prayer

Use this space to write your own reflections.

My Notes:

_____

_____

_____

_____

My Affirmation:

_____

_____

_____

_____

My Prayer:

_____

_____

_____

_____

_____

_____

Testimony Five:

"You Must Have Liked It"

> *"The deepest cuts don't always come from strangers. Sometimes they come from the ones who should have been your shield."*

At sixteen, I still believed home was supposed to be safe. I woke one late summer morning, walked to the front door, and opened it to feel the sun's warmth and the promise of a new day. For a moment, I felt free.

Then I saw them sitting on the couch: my mother's boyfriend and his female cousin. I hadn't even noticed they were there until he spoke.

"You sure look good with that pregnant body and that see-through nightgown."

His words landed like a slap. I froze, my mind racing. See-through? My heart pounded as shame, hot and immediate, surged through me. My stomach churned, as if my body understood it was unsafe long before my brain could catch up.

His cousin's voice sliced through the silence. "You need to stop," she said firmly. "Don't talk to that little girl like that. You know that isn't right."

Her words hung in the air, a small defense, but the damage was done. His comment had turned my own body into something dangerous, something to be ashamed of. In that instant, my sense of safety shattered. But the violation wasn't the hardest part. The hardest part came when I told my mother.

The father of my child, promising to sit beside me, begged me to tell her. So, I gathered what little courage I had, my hands shaking. The child in me still hoped my mother would wrap me in her arms and protect me. With a trembling voice, I told her what her boyfriend had said and how his own cousin had called him out on it.

She looked me in the face, her expression unreadable, and delivered a question that destroyed what was left of my trust: "You must have liked it?"

Those four words didn't just hurt; they rewrote my reality. They taught me that my pain was my fault and that reaching for safety would only lead to blame. My mother wasn't my shield; she was another wound. That day, her question became a dangerous lesson burned into my soul: never expect safety from the ones who should give it most. My body learned it as a permanent tightening in my chest, a flinch in my shoulders. My mind learned to stay small and silent.

It would be years before I could tell that story without bitterness burning my throat. And yet, even in that moment of profound betrayal, a quieter voice whispered to me—God saying, I see you. I believe you. I will not abandon you. That whisper was the first thread of healing, a promise I couldn't yet grasp. Years later, the man who would become my husband stood as the human answer to that promise. He protected me in ways I didn't even know I needed, believing me and choosing me when my own mother had not. Each small act of his protection began to stitch together what her betrayal had torn apart.

Reflection

This moment taught me that the deepest wounds aren't always visible. They're the silent lessons written into our nervous systems and our beliefs about ourselves. From that day forward, I learned to guard my heart and to question the safety of those who should have been my protectors. But I also learned—slowly—that my worth was not defined by what was done to me, nor by who disbelieved me. The shame I carried was never mine to hold. Writing this now is my way of returning it to its rightful owner, reclaiming my story, and affirming that healing is possible —even after betrayal.

> *"Even if my father and mother abandon me, the Lord cares for me."*
> *—Psalm 27:10 (CSB)*

Reader's Guide

Affirmation

I am not defined by the disbelief or betrayal of others. My story is mine, and God holds it with truth and compassion.

 **Prayer:**

God, thank You for being the Parent who never abandons me. Thank You for believing me when others questioned, for protecting me when others failed, and for turning even betrayal into the soil where healing can grow. Strengthen my heart to trust in Your care. Amen.

Reflection Questions:

1. Has someone ever responded to your pain with disbelief? How did it shape your trust?
2. Where in your life do you still carry shame that was never yours to hold?
3. Who has God placed in your life to stand beside you when others abandoned you?

Your Turn: Notes, Affirmation & Personal Prayer

Use this space to write your own reflections.

My Notes:

_____

_____

_____

_____

My Affirmation:

_____

_____

_____

_____

My Prayer:

_____

_____

_____

_____

Testimony Six:

The Choice

> "Sometimes the holiest act of love is to walk away."

By the time I turned twenty-four, the weight of my mother's control had become a crushing burden. Every decision was a battlefield, but my relationship with the man who would become my husband was the final line she refused to let me cross.

She told me I was choosing wrong, even calling me a sell-out because he was white. In her eyes, loving him meant I didn't love her. She twisted affection into a set of conditions, treating family as a prize I could only earn through absolute obedience. But after years of abuse, disbelief, and betrayal, I finally knew I could not survive if I remained bound to her approval. Choosing him was never just about marriage; it was about choosing myself. It was about choosing a love that didn't demand I shrink, and it was my first real stand for freedom from a cycle that had already cost me too much.

The day I left wasn't loud. There were no screaming matches or slammed doors, only the quiet resolve of a young woman who was finally saying, "enough." I knew the cost. I knew I would be branded ungrateful, rebellious, and lost. The truth, however, was that I had been lost for years under her roof. Walking out that door wasn't rebellion—it was a resurrection. And in that choice, I felt God's whisper again: You are not forsaken. You are mine.

But that divine whisper didn't instantly erase the human echo of what I had done. Leaving wasn't a single act; it carried consequences, and the absence of her voice was often louder than her presence had ever been. I wrestled with a profound guilt, wondering if I had walked away too soon or if loyalty demanded I keep enduring. Over time, however, I came to see the truth: staying would have meant shrinking, and shrinking was never what God had planned for me. Her rejection carved new scars, and for years, I expected all belonging to come with strings attached.

This painful separation taught me something essential: love without freedom is not love at all. God never chained me to earn His acceptance, so why should I stay bound to someone who did?

This hard-won understanding carried me into a marriage that would be tested in new ways, a marriage where love had to prove itself stronger than prejudice. Our blended family became a place of healing old wounds while raising children in a world eager to judge. I didn't know then that choosing him was only the first threshold I would cross. There would be others—some joyful, some devastating. But in that moment at twenty-four, it was my first clear act of defiance against the generational chains that had held my family for too long.

> "I call heaven and earth as witnesses against you today that I have set before you life and death, blessing and curse. Choose life so that you and your descendants may live."
> —Deuteronomy 30:19 (CSB)

Reflection

This chapter isn't about abandonment—it's about reclaiming agency. Walking away from dysfunction doesn't make you weak; it means you're honoring what God placed inside you. If you've ever had to leave someone you love in order to survive, know this: that act may be the bravest form of love there is. Love for them, love for truth, and most of all —love for yourself.

Reader's Guide

Affirmation

I have the courage to choose life, even when it costs me comfort, approval, or belonging.

Reflection Questions:

1. What hard choices have you had to make to protect your peace?
2. How do you discern when obedience to God means disobedience to unhealthy people?
3. What generational patterns are you breaking by choosing differently?

 **Prayer:**

God, thank You for teaching me that love does not come through control. Thank You for giving me the courage to walk away from what harmed me and step into the life You planned for me. Strengthen me to continue choosing life—for myself, for my family, and for the generations that come after me. Amen.

Your Turn: Notes, Affirmation & Personal Prayer

Use this space to write your own reflections.

My Notes:

_____

_____

_____

_____

My Affirmation:

_____

_____

_____

_____

My Prayer:

_____

_____

_____

_____

_____

_____

Testimony Seven:

Potpies and New Shoes

> *"We didn't have much, but love made it enough."*

The early years of our marriage were stitched together with struggle and sacrifice. We didn't have fancy dinners or designer clothes; we had frozen potpies bought in bulk—the kind you prayed would stretch through another season because there was no money for gas, no cushion for new shoes, and no backup plan.

There were nights I'd sit on the bed with bills spread out like battle lines. The enemies were always the same: rent, utilities, groceries, the car payment, insurance. No matter how I arranged them, the math never worked. We juggled, stretched, and prayed. Somehow, we always made it through.

What we lacked in financial resources, we made up for with unwavering care. My husband and I stood shoulder to shoulder, determined that our children would never feel the full weight of the burdens we carried. They always had two potpies and rice, a glass of milk, and an apple with every meal—a rule my husband established to keep them nourished. At night, they took a multivitamin before bed. Their plates matched, their routines were steady, and their sense of normalcy remained intact, even when our own survival felt like walking a tightrope.

We learned to turn scarcity into creativity. Handmade decorations became birthday treasures, and laughter filled the gaps left by bare cupboards. On rare, golden days when all three kids had new shoes at the same time, it felt like true wealth. Those moments were never about footwear; they were about dignity. They were about seeing our children walk into the world without lack showing on their faces.

Looking back, I see the profound grace in those years. They were hard—so hard—but they taught me what resilience really looks like. It isn't shiny or glamorous. It's the quiet, ordinary choice to keep going when logic tells you to quit. It's raising children who feel deeply loved even when dinner comes from the freezer section. It's a marriage that doesn't collapse under pressure but bends, flexes, and somehow holds.

Through it all, God's hand was steady. He multiplied the little we had and carried us through seasons when, by all accounts, we should have drowned. Those potpies and shoes became powerful symbols—not of our poverty, but of His provision. I didn't realize it then, but those years of stretching and scraping were a training ground. They were preparing us to endure storms that were not just financial, but emotional, spiritual, and generational. Those lean years taught us resilience, but we would soon learn that faith was the only thing strong enough to carry us through the fires to come.

Reflection

There's a holy kind of strength in showing up, every day, with what little you have—and making it enough. This chapter is about more than potpies and shoes. It's about love in motion, faith under pressure, and the legacy of care we give our children when we make sure they never feel the weight of our struggle. If you're in a season of scraping by, don't underestimate what you're building. Every quiet act of love is a seed. And one day, your children will look back and call it abundance.

> *"My God will supply all your needs according to his riches in glory in Christ Jesus."*
> *—Philippians 4:19 (CSB)*

Affirmation

I honor the seasons of struggle that shaped my strength. God's provision is not always glamorous, but it is always enough.

 **Prayer:**

God, thank You for carrying me through lean seasons. Thank You for showing me that love, creativity, and faith are greater than money alone. Teach me to see Your provision in the small things, and to pass on gratitude and resilience to the generations after me. Amen.

Reflection Questions:

1. What "potpies and shoes" moments do you remember from your own life—the times when provision came in humble packages?
2. How has scarcity shaped your creativity or resilience?
3. How can you honor God today for the ways He has supplied your needs in the past?

Your Turn: Notes, Affirmation & Personal Prayer

Use this space to write your own reflections.

My Notes:

_____

_____

_____

_____

My Affirmation:

_____

_____

_____

_____

My Prayer:

_____

_____

_____

_____

_____

_____

Part II: The Gathering Storm

(Escalation, Conflict, Emotional Buildup)

Trigger Warning: This section contains references to emotional abuse, family conflict, and trauma that may be distressing to some readers.

Prelude

Storms don't arrive all at once; they gather. They begin as whispers, as a tension in the air, as the uneasy feeling that the ground beneath you is shifting. For me, these were the years the pressure began to build. Family fractures widened from hairline cracks into deep chasms. Love became conditional, and survival turned into a full-time job. Yet even as the clouds darkened, I could feel God stirring—not just preparing me to endure the storm but shaping me for something greater than the storm itself.

Testimony Eight:

Breathing Room

"Sometimes peace feels like a borrowed breath."

By the time the kids were grown and starting their own lives, a new kind of quiet settled over the house. The rhythm of life slowed. The bills were still there, but they no longer crushed us. There was food in the pantry, gas in the car, and space to exhale without the familiar clench of panic.

In 2012, my husband and I became grandparents for the first time. Our granddaughter, Leiliana, arrived and turned our world upside down in the best possible way. She was the love of our lives from the very first moment. Holding her, I felt as if God had handed me a living promise—that all the struggles and sacrifices of raising our children had produced something beautiful beyond measure. Leiliana brought laughter back into our home in ways I hadn't realized we were missing. Her giggles could lift the heaviest day, and the sound of her little feet running down the hallway carried more joy than any paycheck.

I found myself treasuring the simplest things: rocking her to sleep, brushing her tiny curls, listening to her string words together as if language were a secret she was letting me in on.

My husband, who had worked so tirelessly to provide, softened in her presence in a way that melted my heart. He would sit on the floor and let her climb all over him as if he were her personal jungle gym. He bought her little shoes even when she hadn't outgrown the old ones, just to see her face light up.

He called her "baby girl" with such pride in his voice that it felt like healing for all the years when survival had left us too tired to notice life's small delights.

With Leiliana, I could finally do what I never had the time or money to do when my own kids were small. I baked cookies without stretching the ingredients. I bought gifts "just because," not only for birthdays or Christmas. I could sit on the floor and simply play, free from the nagging thought of bills stacked on the counter. With her, I was able to experience childhood again—this time through the lens of abundance, not scarcity.

Breathing room doesn't erase the storms that came before it, nor does it guarantee storms won't come again. But it is a gift. For a season, we lived without the sharp edge of scarcity at our heels. We could go out to dinner, laugh without a weight pressing behind the joy, and truly rest. That season was God's reminder that He doesn't only meet us in our crises; He also delights in giving us stillness, allowing us to taste what peace feels like, even if only for a while.

I didn't know then how brief that season would feel, or how desperately I would cling to its memory when the next wave of trials came. But I do know this: those years gave me the strength to keep going. They renewed me. They proved that survival wasn't the only rhythm my life was destined to know. Sometimes, God doesn't just carry us through the fire—He lays us down beside quiet waters and restores our soul.

Reflection

Peace doesn't always come in grand miracles. Sometimes, it arrives in the shape of a child's giggle or the stillness of a house without worry. This chapter is a reminder that healing isn't only about surviving pain, it's also about embracing joy when it finally finds you. If you've walked through long seasons of struggle, hold tight to the quiet ones. They are more than rest—they are restoration.

"He lets me lie down in green pastures; he leads me beside quiet waters. He renews my life."
—Psalm 23:2–3 (CSB)

Affirmation

I welcome seasons of rest as gifts from God, reminders that peace is possible and healing is real.

 **Prayer:**

God, thank You for the quiet seasons, the years when the pressure lifted and I could finally breathe. Thank You for the gift of Leiliana, and the reminder that love multiplies through generations. Help me savor the memories of Your provision and carry that peace with me when storms return. Amen.

Reflection Questions:

1. What season of your life felt like "breathing room"?
2. How do you honor times of peace without fearing their end?
3. What small ways can you create quiet waters in your current life, even in the midst of struggle?

Your Turn: Notes, Affirmation & Personal Prayer

Use this space to write your own reflections.

My Notes:

_____

_____

_____

_____

My Affirmation:

_____

_____

_____

_____

My Prayer:

_____

_____

_____

_____

_____

Testimony Nine:

Three Pages in Michigan

> *"Old wounds have a way of resurfacing in new rooms."*

By 2020, I thought I had finally earned my place. Degrees lined the wall, years of experience stood behind me, and a track record of results spoke for itself. I believed I had proven my worth. Then one day in Michigan, all of that was reduced to a few pages in red ink—and a conference room I'll never forget.

I had turned in a report of over two hundred pages, work that had taken days of focus and long nights to complete. Instead of returning it with feedback, my boss called me into a conference room. With one of my coworkers sitting beside her, she asked me to read the report out loud. At first, I thought she wanted to hear how it flowed, but I quickly realized this wasn't about content. It was about watching me stumble, about exposing what she saw as a weakness.

What cut deepest was that they should have known better. Both were former educators—my boss a classroom teacher, my coworker a special education teacher. Of all people, they understood what dyslexia looks like. They knew the exhaustion of forcing letters into order, the way words can flip themselves on a page. And still, they sat there, waiting for me to prove what they already suspected: that I didn't belong.

Every stumble over a word felt like a gut punch. My throat tightened, my palms began to sweat, and shame wrapped around me like a heavy cloak. It was humiliating, exhausting, and cruel. I just wanted to disappear.

The days that followed were some of the hardest of my professional life. Walking into the office felt like stepping onto a stage where everyone had seen me fail. I second-guessed every email I sent, every document I touched, every meeting I spoke in. Confidence that had taken years to build crumbled in minutes. I found myself shrinking—volunteering less, speaking less, doing everything I could to avoid being noticed. It was the gnawing fear that maybe they were right. Maybe I really didn't belong. But humiliation does not get the last word. Slowly, sometimes painfully, I began to rebuild.

At first, it was small things: reading a page out loud at home to remind myself that stumbling wasn't failing. Reminding myself that dyslexia was not a deficiency but a difference—that my brain processed information in ways that were challenging in one setting but powerful in another. I leaned into the gifts it gave me: creativity, problem-solving, and the ability to see patterns others missed.

I started praying differently, too. Not just, "God, help me survive this job," but "God, remind me who I am when this job makes me forget." Scripture became my anchor. Psalm 118:22 whispered to me in the quiet:

"The stone that the builders rejected has become the cornerstone."

I leaned on the people who truly saw me. My husband reminded me that one room, one boss, and one coworker did not define me. My children reminded me that my voice mattered. And every time Leiliana's little arms wrapped around my neck, I felt God whispering: *You are more than enough.*

Piece by piece, my confidence returned. I stopped seeing dyslexia as an enemy and began to embrace it as part of my God-given design. I realized that the very thing people used to tear me down had also made me strong, empathetic, and resilient. That day in the conference room scarred me, yes. But scars don't mean you are broken; they mean you have healed.

What others used as a weapon, God was already shaping into a testimony. They thought they were tearing me down, but He was building me into something stronger.

The storm was gathering, yes.

But so was my strength.

Reflection

The deepest wounds aren't always from strangers. Sometimes they wear titles and degrees and sit across from you in polished rooms. But your value isn't up for debate. Not then. Not now. If you've ever been made to feel small in a place where you were called to rise, I hope this reminds you: rejection doesn't define you. Resilience does. And the very stone they reject may be the cornerstone God uses to rebuild your next chapter.

> *"The stone that the builders rejected has become the cornerstone."*
> —Psalm 118:22 (CSB)

Reader's Guide

Affirmation

I am not defined by humiliation or rejection. What others dismiss, God redeems.

 **Prayer:**

God, thank You for being with me in rooms where I felt small. Thank You for turning my stumbles into strength and my wiring into wisdom. Remind me daily that my value is not in flawless performance, but in Your purpose for my life. Amen.

Reflection Questions:

1. When have you been forced to "perform" in a way that exposed your deepest vulnerabilities?
2. How did the aftermath of that moment affect your confidence or sense of belonging?
3. What small steps can you take today to rebuild confidence where shame once lived?
4. In what ways has God turned what others called weakness into a cornerstone in your life?

Your Turn: Notes, Affirmation & Personal Prayer

Use this space to write your own reflections.

My Notes:

_____

_____

_____

_____

My Affirmation:

_____

_____

_____

_____

My Prayer:

_____

_____

_____

_____

Testimony
Ten:

Crossing Thresholds

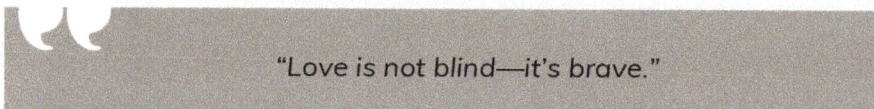

"Love is not blind—it's brave."

By the time I married my husband, I knew life with him would mean crossing thresholds other people weren't ready for. He was white; I was Black. He was six years older; I was a young mother raising three children. On paper, it didn't look like a fairytale. To some, it looked like it shouldn't work at all.

But love isn't math, or a list of pros and cons. Love is a choice you make every day, especially when the world has an opinion about your right to make it.

Over the years, we faced quiet judgments, sideways looks, and unspoken questions. People made assumptions about me because I was Black, about him because he was white, and about us because we were together. At times, it felt like we weren't just carrying a marriage; we were carrying the weight of everyone else's prejudice. And yet, through every struggle and storm that could have split us apart, we kept choosing each other. He wasn't perfect, and neither was I. But we were both willing to fight—not against each other, but for each other.

Crossing thresholds also meant blending a family. My husband didn't just choose me; he chose my children. He stepped into fatherhood when they were young, becoming the steady hand at the dinner table and the provider when money was thin. He helped with homework, sat through parent-teacher conferences, and took them to doctor's appointments when I couldn't call off work. He carried responsibilities he never had to, but chose to, anyway.

More than that, he taught them how to navigate a world that would not always be gentle. He sat with our son, a young Black man, and prepared him for the reality that society had already drawn conclusions about who he was. His words shaped them, protected them, and still echo in how they walk through the world today.

One moment in 2006, when we were living in Hillsboro, Oregon, crystallizes this reality. He took our son to a doctor's appointment. At the front desk, the receptionist slid a HIPAA form across the counter for our son to sign.

My husband calmly said, **"I'll sign it—he's a minor."**

Without looking up, she dismissed him. "Sir, you're obviously not his father."

He didn't raise his voice, but he stood his ground. After having our son sit down, he asked to speak with the manager. Then he called me at work— not because he needed me to fix it, but because he knew how deeply the disrespect would wound me. Even with legal adoption papers, even after years of being their dad, a stranger's glance could attempt to erase his role.

I was hurt for them both: for my son, who had to witness his father's role being questioned, and for my husband, who had worked so hard to make our children feel secure. But I was also angry at the casual disrespect that cuts so much deeper in a biracial family, where acceptance is never guaranteed.

family, where acceptance is never guaranteed.

That moment was a stark reminder of the courage it takes to cross thresholds. My husband could have walked away years earlier, but he stayed. He fought for them. He fought for us. He taught our children that real love isn't measured by bloodlines or public approval, but by the daily act of showing up.

Looking back, I know we crossed thresholds many people would never dare. It wasn't easy, but I wouldn't trade it. Love across difference is not weakness.

It is resilience.

It is faith with skin on.

It is the daily "yes."

Reflection

True love is not about ignoring difference, it's about honoring it. This chapter is a tribute to every couple, every blended family, every parent who chose love across thresholds of race, blood, background, or judgment. If you've ever been questioned for who you love or how you love, may this remind you: the world doesn't get to define the power of your bond. Your courage, your commitment, your care, that's the legacy you're building.

> *"Above all, put on love, which is the perfect bond of unity."*
> —Colossians 3:14 (CSB)

Reader's Guide

Affirmation

I honor the love that crosses boundaries, defies expectations, and reflects God's unity.

Prayer:

God, thank You for teaching me that love is an act of courage. Strengthen me to keep choosing to love even when it's hard, even when others don't understand, and even when the world tries to divide what You have joined. Amen.

Reflection Questions:

1. What thresholds have you had to cross in love or relationships?
2. How do you stay rooted when others misunderstand or judge your choices?
3. What has love taught you about resilience?

Your Turn: Notes, Affirmation & Personal Prayer

Use this space to write your own reflections.

My Notes:

_____

_____

_____

_____

My Affirmation:

_____

_____

_____

_____

My Prayer:

_____

_____

_____

_____

_____

Part III: The Fire

(The Breaking Point, Transformation)

Trigger Warning: This section contains references to workplace trauma, medical distress, and suicidal ideation. Please care for yourself as you read and pause if needed. You are not alone.

Prelude

The fire came suddenly—and yet, I had been standing in smoke for years. This was the season of breaking, when everything I had built in strength and silence began to collapse. My career, my body, my faith, and my sense of safety were all tested in ways I could never have imagined.

But the fire, though devastating, was never meant to destroy me. It was meant to purify, to burn away everything I thought I was, so that I could finally become who God created me to be.

Testimony Eleven:

The Cost of Obedience

"Obedience will cost you everything—except your soul."

I used to believe that obeying God meant things would get easier. That if I followed the whisper of His voice, He would reward that trust with peace and restoration. So, in 2021, I relocated to Washington to be closer to my family. I left a steady life because I believed He was calling me into something redemptive.

But what I stepped into was not healing. It was abandonment.
I had uprooted everything for them—my mother, my sister, my brother, my children, and my grandchildren. I thought proximity would finally mean closeness; instead, it only revealed how distant we had always been. By 2022, the cracks had widened into chasms. One afternoon, they were reminiscing about a beautiful day trip, laughing and sharing the warm memory. I asked, "Why didn't you invite me?"

My mother and sister looked at me. "We thought you were too busy with school."

Yes, I was in the middle of my doctoral program. But my schedule never stopped them from calling when they needed something—HR problems, forms filled out, family crises. They always knew how to find me when I was useful. But for joy? For simple inclusion? I wasn't even an afterthought. It felt like Cinderella watching the ball from the ashes, while all the refrains of "we just want what's best for you" rang hollow.

Then came the phone call that changed everything.

Early one morning, my daughter Felisha called, and I could hear the fracture in her voice. She told me what my sister—her aunt—had done. The suitcase. The stairs. The basement floor. The cruel, humiliating games that turned meals into punishment. And then she said it wasn't just her. My other children had endured it, too, and had kept silent for years to protect me.

My world tilted. My breath stopped. I had been working, studying, trusting my family to care for my babies while I fought to build a better life for us all. And behind my back, they had made that life a living hell.

With my cousin Felicia on the line for support, I called my mother. When I told her what our children had finally shared, her first question was, "Do you believe her?"

My own mother. Asking if I believed my own child. The silence on the line was her answer. No defense. No grief. No heartbreak for her grandchildren. Just nothing.

Days passed. Then my sister went public on social media, posting a challenge for all to see:

"You know where I live. The door is wide open. Come beat my ass like you said you would."

And that was it. The final, undeniable proof. I was not a daughter or a sister. I was just someone useful—now inconvenient because I had finally woken up. So, I removed myself—quietly, prayerfully, and permanently.

It was Felicia who stood by me when the ground collapsed. It was my husband who saw the toll it took on my body and spirit, even when I tried to hide it. Their presence didn't erase the loss, but it reminded me I wasn't completely alone.

In the aftermath, a new resolve took root.

I will not carry the weight of vengeance. I will carry the weight of healing— For me. For my children. For the generations after me.

I can't undo what was done to them. But I can help them heal.

And I can finally admit: it was never my fault for working hard to give them a better life. It was theirs for destroying what I trusted them to protect.

The breathing room didn't last. What felt like stability gave way to cracks I could no longer ignore. I didn't know it yet, but the fire was coming. And this time, it wouldn't just scorch the surface. It would test the very core of who I was.

Reflection

Sometimes obedience doesn't lead to immediate peace. Sometimes, it leads you straight into the fire. But even in that fire, God refines. This chapter is for anyone who chose love, only to be met with betrayal. Who followed God's voice, only to walk into silence. Your pain is not proof that you failed, it's proof that you stepped into truth. And even when the people you trusted fall away, God does not. He sees. He cares. And He is already making something holy out of your ashes.

> *"Even if my father and mother abandon me, the Lord cares for me."*
> *—Psalm 27:10 (CSB)*

Reader's Guide

Affirmation

I will not carry the weight of vengeance. I will carry the weight of healing.

 **Prayer:**

God, I release the pain of betrayal—the kind that came dressed as love. I give You the heartbreak, the rage, the grief, and the shame. Thank You for opening my eyes. Thank You for giving me the strength to walk away and the courage to believe my children. Help me break every generational curse of silence, abuse, and denial. I choose healing. I choose truth. I choose You. Amen.

Reflection Questions:

1. When did clarity about someone's true character finally set you free?
2. What does it cost to protect your peace and your children's healing?
3. How do you grieve the family you wanted, while letting go of the one you had?

Your Turn: Notes, Affirmation & Personal Prayer

Use this space to write your own reflections.

My Notes:

_____

_____

_____

_____

My Affirmation:

_____

_____

_____

_____

My Prayer:

_____

_____

_____

_____

_____

_____

Testimony
Twelve:

Faith in the Fire

> *"I didn't just walk through fire—I worked in it, lived in it, and prayed through it with ashes still on my skin."*

There are fires you step into by choice and fires you are thrown into. My job was the latter. I became responsible for investigating trauma in the workplace—trauma that left people broken, violated, and silenced. I watched employees die on video. I listened to disclosures of rape and prostitution that happened at work. I carried the weight of stories that would never appear in any policy manual, wearing them like invisible but heavy layers.

I was supposed to hold it all together. Be calm, be professional, be neutral. But no one ever asked if I was okay. No one checked for the cracks forming within me.

Then the trauma I managed within office walls began to spill into my own life. In 2024, the calls for help grew louder, the deadlines tighter, and the support thinner. My boss—narcissistic, sharp, and unyielding—didn't care who broke in the process. She once said, "I don't give a damn about anyone. I have a job to do—that's why I get paid the big bucks." That was her leadership philosophy: survival of the coldest.

At home, my husband saw what I refused to admit. He watched me work until dawn, snapping at him, carrying my laptop like a life raft I couldn't let go of. "I hate your boss. I hate your job," he told me one night, his voice firm and pained. At the time, I brushed it off as frustration. Now, I see he was grieving the version of me he was losing to the fire.

Every email and phone call felt like another spark on dry timber. I kept thinking: *if I just prayed harder, worked longer, sacrificed more, God would deliver me.* But faith doesn't always pull you out of the fire. Sometimes, it holds you steady while you burn.

I clung to scripture in the silence between investigations, whispering its promises like lifelines over my fracturing soul. But I felt scorched. I felt consumed. I felt utterly alone.

Still, a part of me knew: if God brought me to this, He would not abandon me in it. The fire wasn't meant to kill me. It was meant to reveal what could not be destroyed.

Reflection

There is a sacred kind of strength in being broken where others are broken. This chapter isn't about surviving despite faith—it's about enduring through it. If you've ever felt consumed by the very work you were called to do, know this: the fire may leave you singed, but it does not have the final say. Your faith is not meant to spare you storms—but to carry you through them with more of yourself left intact than you ever knew possible.

> "When you pass through the waters, I will be with you, and the rivers will not overwhelm you. When you walk through the fire, you will not be scorched, and the flame will not burn you."
> —Isaiah 43:2 (CSB)

Reader's Guide

Affirmation

Even in the fire, God is with me. What burns away is not my identity but the lies that tried to bind me.

 **Prayer:**

God, you see the fires I've walked through—the ones I chose and the ones I never asked for. Thank You for sustaining me when I felt consumed. Thank You for keeping my soul intact when everything else around me turned to ash. Help me trust that even the fire is not wasted in Your hands. Amen.

Reflection Questions:

1. What fires have you walked through that felt unbearable?
2. How did you sense God's presence, even when you felt scorched?
3. What lies or burdens have the fire burned away, leaving only what's true?

Use this space to write your own reflections.

My Notes:

_____

_____

_____

_____

My Affirmation:

_____

_____

_____

_____

My Prayer:

_____

_____

_____

_____

_____

_____

Testimony
Thirteen:

Choosing Sanity

"There comes a moment when survival means laying your work down before it buries you."

By 2024, the cracks in my life had become canyons. Every day at my job felt like walking into a war zone, but the battle was invisible, the wounds were silent, and the damage was embedding itself in my nervous system. I was drowning, and no one in power cared if I surfaced.

It began with my request for accommodation. Dyslexia, dysgraphia, ADHD —conditions that didn't make me incapable, they simply meant I needed different tools to do my job. Instead of support, I received mockery. My boss offered "solutions" that felt like insults: *Change the background color on your screen. Use the company chatbot.* Then came the dagger: "Your disability might cost you your job." I swallowed the words, but the bitterness remained.

Then my body began its own betrayal. On **October 24, 2024,** I sat in a doctor's office with my husband, listening as the words *bilateral carpal tunnel* and *cubital tunnel* hit the air. My hands, the very tools of my work, were burning and aching. Stress had finally etched itself into my flesh.

A week later, the world itself shattered. **October 31, 2024**—the Vancouver Mall shooting. I was inside when the bullets rang out. I heard the screams and the chaos of bodies running in every direction. The terror in their eyes carved itself into mine. The external chaos now matched the internal one.

I tried to return to work on **January 27, 2025,** but logging back in felt like stepping into a coffin. The dread was immediate. Nothing had changed; if anything, it was worse. Then came the ER visit on **February 7, 2025.** I hadn't felt chest pain, only nausea, dizziness, and the ache of a body screaming that something was wrong. My blood pressure read 151/102. The doctors sent me home with Tylenol, never mentioning the truth printed on my discharge.

papers: *possible inferior infarct.* Another system failure. Another betrayal.

And then, on **February 28,** the final blow: the performance review.

"Communication issues. Missed deadlines. Quality concerns."

Each phrase was a verdict, erasing every denied accommodation and every sleepless night of trauma. I wasn't seen as a person drowning; I was painted as a defective employee.

That night, something inside me finally broke—not in despair, but in clarity. I heard my husband's words from months before echo in my mind: "I hate your boss. I hate your job." He had named the truth long before I could admit it. He saw what the fire was doing to me, and he was right.

I looked out the window of my home in Battle Ground, the silence pressing in, and finally said it out loud: "I can't do this anymore."
It wasn't a surrender to defeat; it was a surrender to God, who had been whispering for months: *Lay it down. Choose life. Choose sanity.*

So, I picked up the phone and made the call. I began the intake process for a 60-day Partial Hospitalization Program. It was the scariest and holiest decision I have ever made—to stop breaking and finally let myself be healed. When doubt crept in, it was Felicia's voice that steadied me, a reminder from God that choosing help wasn't weakness—it was the ultimate act of strength.

> *"Come to me, all of you who are weary and burdened, and I will give you rest."*
> *—Matthew 11:28 (CSB)*

Reflection: The Holy Work of Stopping

There comes a time when obedience looks like stopping instead of striving. For years, I believed rest had to be earned and that healing would come only after I had proven my endurance. But the truth is, exhaustion doesn't honor God—obedience does. When God says, lay it down, it's not a suggestion. It's a rescue.

The culture around us glorifies burnout and calls it excellence. But burnout is not holy—it's bondage. True faith sometimes looks like walking away from what breaks you, even when others call it quitting. Choosing sanity, choosing peace, choosing rest—these are sacred acts of resistance against a world that rewards self-destruction.

When I finally surrendered my job, I discovered something unexpected: the world didn't end. I did not lose myself. I simply found the part of me that had been whispering beneath the noise all along.

Healing begins when the hurry ends.

 Closing Note

When my strength felt gone, Felicia reminded me that choosing help was not weakness—it was courage. Her voice became proof that I didn't have to survive alone. Sometimes God anchors you through people, even before you realize how much you'll need them.

Affirmation

Choosing sanity is not weakness—it is strength. My healing is holy work.

 **Prayer:**

God, thank You for meeting me in the breaking point. Thank You for reminding me that I am not required to burn out to prove my worth. Teach me to rest in You, to lay down what destroys me, and to trust that healing is the work You bless. Amen.

Reflection Questions:

1. What has your body or spirit been telling you that you can no longer ignore?
2. How do you know when it's time to lay something down?
3. What step toward sanity is God asking you to take today?

Testimony
Fourteen:

The Eyes in the Back of My Mind

"I'm not paranoid. I'm patterned."

People think trauma ends when the event is over. They assume that once the danger has passed, the body should relax, and the mind should forget. But trauma doesn't operate on a calendar; it operates on memory. And my memory doesn't live only in my mind. It lives in my muscles, my pulse, and the constant scanning of my eyes.

Sometimes I'll be at home, reading or working, and I'll suddenly feel a presence, as if someone just ran past the window. My logical brain knows no one is there, but my nervous system doesn't care. It's already activated. My breathing shifts, my eyes scan the room, and I check the locks on the doors. In public, it's even harder. Every store, parking lot, and restaurant is a potential danger zone. I look for exits. I scan faces. I watch hands and pockets, wondering who might be carrying a gun. Not because I want to, but because my body insists on it.

When someone gets too close, I flinch. A part of me wants to yell or run— not out of rudeness, but out of an instinct carved by experience. My body doesn't trust proximity. It remembers being unsafe.

That's what people don't understand about PTSD and C-PTSD: it's not about being "dramatic" or "too sensitive." It's about having a body that learned to survive—and doesn't yet know how to stop.

By September 2025, I had already been through three rounds of Partial Hospitalization Programs and two rounds of Intensive Outpatient Programs. Nearly a year of my life had been dedicated to treatment: structured days, therapy groups, doctor visits, and endless hours of unpacking pain. And still, trauma showed up uninvited.

Early that month, six months after I had gone on medical leave, I was sitting in my living room when I thought I saw a figure race past the back window. My heart spiked. I grabbed my phone and checked the cameras—nothing. My husband went outside to look—no one. We looked at each other, both realizing it at the same time: a PTSD episode was visiting, an unwelcome guest settling in for the night. It didn't matter if the window was shut, or the doors were locked. My body still believed danger was near.

That night, I realized something both painful and freeing: healing isn't erasure. Healing is learning to live with the echoes until they finally fade.

And so, I keep learning. Slowly, gently, with therapy, prayer, grounding exercises, and radical self-compassion. I remind myself: You're not there anymore.

And some days, I believe it.

Reflection: Living With the Echoes

Healing from trauma is not about forgetting—it's about remembering differently. The echoes don't mean you're broken; they mean your body is still trying to protect you. Survival taught your nervous system to be on guard, and it takes time and tenderness to unlearn that vigilance.

I used to hate my body for overreacting—for trembling, for scanning, for mistaking safety for danger. But now I see it differently. My body was never my enemy; it was my soldier. It kept me alive when the world was unsafe. The problem wasn't my vigilance—it was that no one had ever told my body it was okay to stand down.

Faith has become my ultimate grounding tool. When flashbacks come, I speak truth over fear.

When my heart races, I breathe in the name of Jesus, letting it fill the space where panic used to live. I remind myself that the God who carried me through the fire also stands guard after the fire.

Healing is not pretending the eyes in the back of my mind don't exist; it's training them to see light instead of danger. Every calm breath is an act of rebellion against trauma's grip. Every moment of peace is proof that the past does not get to define the present.

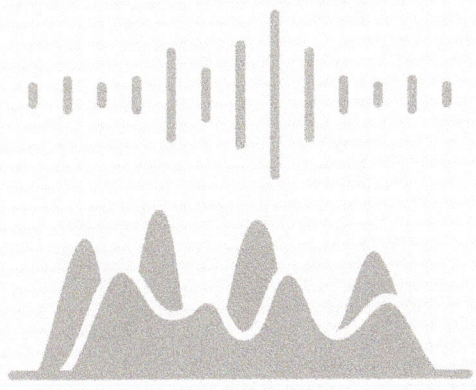

Affirmation

I honor my body's patterns, but I remind myself daily: I am safe.

 **Prayer:**

God, you see the patterns trauma has written into my body. Thank You for never abandoning me in those moments when my fear doesn't make sense to others. Teach me to calm the storms inside me. Restore my sense of safety—not just around me, but within me. Amen.

Reflection Questions:

1. When has your body reacted to fear before your mind could make sense of it?
2. How do you create safety for yourself in spaces where you feel vulnerable?
3. What practices help you remind your nervous system that you are not in danger anymore?

Use this space to write your own reflections.

My Notes:

_____

_____

_____

_____

My Affirmation:

_____

_____

_____

_____

My Prayer:

_____

_____

_____

_____

_____

Testimony Fifteen:

Felicia, My Anchor

"Sometimes, the mother you needed is disguised as the cousin God gave you."

Felicia has always been there. Not just sometimes, and not only when it was convenient. Always.

We are only five years apart, yet she has cared for me like a mother from the very beginning. When I think of a love that wraps around your broken places and stays—even when it's hard—it's her face that comes to mind. She is my cousin by blood, my sister by choice, and my mother in the ways that mattered most. She was there when all three of my children were born, holding space and whispering encouragement. She never missed a moment. That's who she is: quietly fierce, loyal beyond words, and present in a way you never have to ask for. She just knows.

People used to call her the "mean cousin," but they never saw the truth. They didn't see the way she put herself last, again and again, to make sure everyone else was okay. They didn't see her in ER rooms, on late-night phone calls, or in whispered prayers. Nursing wasn't just a profession she chose—it was who she already was. She had been caring for people long before anyone paid her to do it.

In early November 2024, when my body and mind collapsed, the suicidal ideation was louder than my will to live. I was drowning in silence, but Felicia saw me. She knew something was wrong before I could speak it. And as always, she showed up—not with judgment, but with tenderness; not with fear, but with presence.

Felicia has been my anchor. The one I could always call, the one I never had to explain myself to. She has walked through her own storms, and I pray one day she lets God use her voice the way He has nudged me to use mine. Even now, I feel the pull to protect her as she has always protected me. She is not just part of my story; she is part of my survival. She is proof that family doesn't always fail you. Sometimes, they save you.

Fire doesn't leave anything untouched. By the time the flames died down, the life I had built was gone, and the person I once was had been burned away. For a while, I thought I was standing in ruins. But slowly, I realized: resurrection doesn't begin when everything is intact. It begins when you have nothing left but God, and He whispers, rise.

> "Two are better than one because they have a good reward for their efforts. For if either falls, his companion can lift him up."
> —Ecclesiastes 4:9–10 (CSB)

Reflection: The Ministry of Presence

There are people God sends into our lives who don't need titles to make an impact—they carry quiet ministries in their very presence. Felicia's love was never loud; it was steady. It didn't demand attention; it offered it. She didn't save me with grand speeches; she saved me with her nearness, her knowing, her unspoken "I've got you."

For years, I searched for a love that was perfect—clean, easy, and unconditional. But what I learned through Felicia is that real love is often messy. It shows up in emergency rooms and sits beside you in silence when words can't hold the weight. It is loyal not because it's convenient, but because it's covenant. Her love taught me that God doesn't just heal us through miracles; He heals us through people who embody His faithfulness. Sometimes your anchor isn't a supernatural act; it's the person God places beside you who simply refuses to let go.

Affirmation

I honor the gift of chosen family. God has placed anchors in my life who keep me steady when I feel adrift.

 **Prayer:**

God, thank You for the gift of chosen family—the ones who show up without being asked, who love without condition, and who stay when others leave. Thank You for Felicia. Bless her. Strengthen her. Remind her that the love she gives is seen, felt, and deeply honored.

And help me to be for her what she has always been for me—an anchor. Amen.

Reflection Questions:

1. Who has God used in your life to show you a different kind of love?
2. What relationships have been a lifeline in your darkest seasons?
3. How can you honor the people who cared for you by also caring for them?
4. How might you become an anchor for someone else?

Use this space to write your own reflections.

My Notes:

_____

_____

_____

_____

My Affirmation:

_____

_____

_____

_____

My Prayer:

_____

_____

_____

_____

_____

_____

Part IV: The Resurrection

(Rebuilding, Healing, Rebirth)

Note: This section explores healing, faith, and restoration. While it references past trauma, its focus is on renewal, hope, and grace.

Prelude

After every fire comes the silence—and then, slowly, the sound of breath returning. Resurrection is not a single moment of triumph; it is a daily rising. It is the gentle work of learning to live again, to rebuild from the ashes, and to trust that the same God who carried me through darkness is now teaching me to walk in the light.

This final section is not about perfection. It's about grace, restoration, and the sacred journey of becoming whole.

Testimony Sixteen:

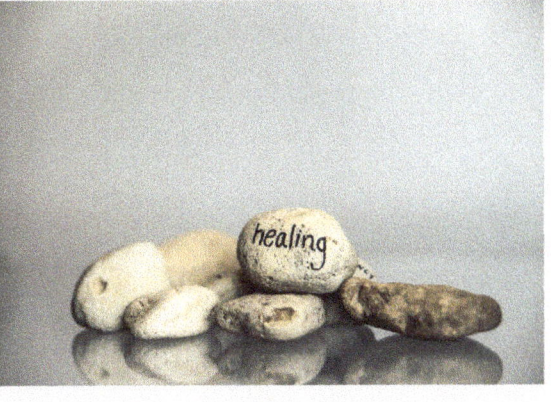

Restoration Is a Process

> "Healing is not a straight line. It's a daily choice."

When I finally laid my work down in March 2025 and entered the Partial Hospitalization Program, I thought healing might come quickly. Sixty days sounded like a long time, and I was desperate to feel better. I imagined myself walking out restored, whole, and ready to begin again.

But healing is not a switch you flip; it is a process—slow, uneven, and humbling. Some days I woke with hope; on others, I couldn't stop crying. Therapy peeled back layers I didn't know I had buried, and group discussions held up mirrors I wasn't always ready to face. Still, through every jagged step, God's hand steadied me.

I learned practical tools: grounding exercises for when my body screamed danger, cognitive reframing for when my thoughts turned cruel, and breathing techniques for when panic tried to steal my air. I practiced radical honesty, naming aloud what I had carried in silence for decades. It was the kind of hard work that left me drained but, somehow, lighter.

I remember sitting in a circle of chairs in group therapy, the air thick with exhaustion. Every face in that room carried its own storm. We weren't polished or pretending—just broken people telling the truth. When my turn came, my voice shook as I admitted I didn't know if I wanted to keep fighting. Silence settled over the room, heavy and knowing. Then one woman whispered, "Me too." And just like that, the shame cracked open.

That moment didn't fix me, but it reminded me that healing doesn't grow in isolation; it grows when pain is met with understanding.

When PHP ended, I moved into Intensive Outpatient Therapy—nine hours a week of groups and reflection. At times it felt endless, like I was circling the same mountain over and over. But each lap was building something inside me: resilience, clarity, and a strength I hadn't known before. By the time I had completed more than 190 days of therapy, I realized restoration wasn't a destination. It was happening in me, day by day, choice by choice.

Others saw it, too. My husband, who had watched me wither, began to notice the small changes: a smile returning, my laughter echoing in the house again. Even my faith community, though they didn't know the details, told me they could see the light returning. Their witness reminded me that healing is not only something you feel; it is something others can see taking shape in you.

Restoration is not one moment of triumph. It is the decision to keep moving, even when you stumble. It is trusting that the same God who carried me through the fire is now teaching me how to live unafraid of the ashes.

> "I am sure of this, that he who started a good work in you will carry it on to completion until the day of Christ Jesus." - Philippians 1:6 (CSB)

> "Therefore, we do not give up. Even though our outer person is being destroyed, our inner person is being renewed day by day." - 2 Corinthians 4:16 (CSB)

Reflection: The Slow Work of God

In a world that celebrates speed, healing often feels like an act of rebellion. We want the miracle without the process—the arrival without the waiting. But God is not in a hurry. He restores what's broken in layers and rhythms, in slow, sacred work that cannot be rushed.

There were days I wanted to skip the process, to jump from pain to peace. But the truth is, the middle is where the transformation happens. It's where grace teaches us endurance and where faith learns to breathe again. Restoration isn't about perfection; it's about presence. It's choosing to show up for yourself in the same way God keeps showing up for you—faithful, patient, and unafraid of your process.

When I think of restoration now, I don't imagine a flawless version of myself. I imagine a softer one. A woman at peace with her progress, who knows that slow healing is still holy healing.

Restoration Is a Process — Closing Reflection

Restoration doesn't erase the evidence of what I've endured—it reframes it. The cracks in me don't signal failure; they mark the places where God's light entered. Healing has taught me to stop rushing the rhythm and start trusting the process. Some days, progress whispers instead of shouts, but even whispers count in heaven. Restoration is not becoming who I used to be, it's becoming who I was always meant to be.

Reader's Guide

Affirmation

I embrace healing as a process. Every step forward, no matter how small, is holy progress.

 **Prayer:**

God, thank You for reminding me that restoration doesn't happen all at once. Thank You for walking with me through every layer of pain and every step toward wholeness. Help me honor the process, trust Your timing, and celebrate the small victories along the way.
Amen.

Reflection Questions:

1. What expectations have you carried about how healing "should" look?
2. How can you show yourself grace on days when the process feels slow?
3. What is one daily practice that helps you move toward restoration?
4. Who has witnessed your healing and reminded you how far you've come?

Your Turn: Notes, Affirmation & Personal Prayer

Use this space to write your own reflections.

My Notes:

_____

_____

_____

_____

My Affirmation:

_____

_____

_____

_____

My Prayer:

_____

_____

_____

_____

Testimony Seventeen:

Love, War, and the Mirror

> *"Marriage is not just love—it is war, reflection, and the daily choice to stay."*

Twenty plus years into a marriage, you would think you've seen it all. You think the biggest battles are behind you and that love will eventually smooth into something easy. But real marriage, the kind that lasts, doesn't work that way. My husband and I have lived through storms together and storms between us, but the fire I walked through with my family and my job didn't just scar me; it scarred us.

Trauma leaks. It seeps into the spaces where intimacy should be safe, and mirrors back the unhealed parts of you in the person lying beside you. He saw the toll long before I was willing to admit it. "I hate your boss, and I hate your job," he told me one night, his voice firm and pained. He was watching me disappear, piece by piece. Though he couldn't fix it, he named what I was too ashamed to confess: I was breaking. This was the same man who had stepped into fatherhood without hesitation all those years ago, and now he was fighting for the woman he had chosen.

Then, in 2025, in the middle of my intensive healing, one Facebook post cracked us wide open. I wrote my truth—about the mall shooting, about the trauma, about the unraveling. I wrote it to free myself. But when he read it, he felt betrayed. To him, my words had turned our private struggle into a public wound. His anger was sharp; his silence, sharper. For days, we circled each other like strangers.

That's the thing about marriage: it forces you to look in the mirror, especially when you'd rather turn away. The conflict revealed the fractures we had ignored, the ways we had stopped listening, and the pain we had allowed to pile up in silence.

Marriage is not just soft words and shared laughter. It is the hard conversations no one wants to have. It is forgiveness and frustration breathing the same air. It is holding your ground one moment and surrendering the next. It is deciding to stay even when the reflection staring back at you feels unbearable.

And through it all, God whispers: Covenant is not convenience. Covenant is a choice. Love is not found; it is forged. Every day, we choose the war, we choose the love, and we choose each other—sometimes in that order.

> "Be completely humble and gentle; be patient, bearing with one another in love."
> —Ephesians 4:2 (CSB)

Reflection: When Love Meets the Mirror

Marriage has a way of holding up a mirror—not to your partner, but to you. It shows you your triggers, your impatience, your pride, and your unhealed places. While it's easier to blame or retreat, God uses that mirror not to shame you, but to refine you.

When my husband and I faced that silence, I realized that love requires immense courage—to listen when you're hurt and to keep reaching when resentment is building walls. Healing within a marriage doesn't always mean returning to what was; sometimes, it means building something new on the ashes of what burned. Love doesn't survive by avoiding the mirror. It survives by looking in it—together—and saying, "Let's try again.

Affirmation

Marriage is not easy, but it is holy. I choose to love daily, even when it costs me comfort.

Prayer:

God, thank You for the gift of covenant love. Thank You for teaching me patience, forgiveness, and humility through marriage. Help me to see my spouse not as an enemy, but as a mirror. Strengthen us to fight not against each other, but for each other—with You at the center. Amen.

Reflection Questions:

1. How has marriage (or a close relationship) mirrored parts of yourself you didn't want to face?
2. What does it mean to choose to love daily, even when it's difficult?
3. Where is God asking you to practice humility, patience, or forgiveness in your closest relationships?
4. What does "forged love" look like in your life today?

Your Turn: Notes, Affirmation & Personal Prayer

Use this space to write your own reflections.

My Notes:

_____

_____

_____

_____

My Affirmation:

_____

_____

_____

_____

My Prayer:

_____

_____

_____

_____

_____

Testimony
Eighteen:

The Mask and the Mirror

"For years, I survived by hiding. Now, I live by revealing."

I wore the mask for so long I almost forgot it wasn't my face. The mask of competence, of perfection, of the "strong Black woman" who could endure anything without breaking. It kept me safe. It kept me employed. It kept me included in spaces that didn't truly want me, only what I could give.

But the mirror never lies. Behind closed doors, I saw the cracks in the facade, the exhaustion, and the shame of trying to keep up with a world not built for the way my brain works. Dyslexia, dysgraphia, ADHD—for decades, I treated them like flaws to be hidden instead of truths to be honored.

At my last job, the mask became unbearable. I needed accommodations, not pity; tools, not dismissal. But instead of support, I was told my disability might cost me my job. I realized then that the mask was not protecting me —it was suffocating me.

So, I took it off. Piece by piece. In therapy, in prayer, in conversations with my children and my husband. I began to write my story not as a victim, but as a woman learning to rise.

The mirror still startles me sometimes. Seeing myself clearly means facing both the wounds and the resilience. It means admitting how much I've lost while also claiming how much I've overcome. It means saying aloud: I am neurodivergent, I am not broken, and I am worthy of every accommodation, every opportunity, and every ounce of respect.

God never asked me to wear a mask; He asked me to live in truth. And now, when I look in the mirror, I no longer see someone failing to measure up. I see a woman God carried through fire and into freedom.

> "You will know the truth, and the truth will set you free."
> —John 8:32 (CSB)

> "The one who started a good work in you will carry it on to completion until the day of Christ Jesus."
> —Philippians 1:6 (CSB)

The Mask and the Mirror — Closing Reflection

The mirror no longer scares me. It reflects both my fragility and my strength, and I've learned to honor both. For years, I performed to be accepted, but freedom came when I stopped auditioning for love and started living in truth. The woman I see now is no longer hiding behind survival; she is breathing in authenticity. Every day I live unmasked, I live closer to the woman God created me to be.

Affirmation

I no longer hide behind masks. I honor the truth of who God made me to be.

Prayer:

God, thank You for removing the masks I once thought I needed to survive. Thank You for showing me that the truth of who I am is not shameful but sacred. Help me to live boldly, without apology, trusting that my freedom is found in Your truth. Amen.

Reflection Questions:

1. What masks have you worn to survive, and what has it cost you?
2. How does it feel to look in the mirror and see your true self both the wounds and the strengths?
What truth about yourself today in order to live more freely?

Use this space to write your own reflections.

My Notes:

_____

_____

_____

_____

My Affirmation:

_____

_____

_____

_____

My Prayer:

_____

_____

_____

_____

_____

Testimony Nineteen:

The Resurrection of Me

> "What they tried to bury, God raised back to life."

Resurrection is not a single, triumphant moment. It is the slow, steady work of learning to breathe again after the fire has passed. The last few years have been a journey through breaking and healing—a process of walking away from what harms, choosing sanity, and surrendering to the slow work of God. The woman who entered that fire is not the one who has emerged. What was buried under the weight of trauma, I can now say God is raising back to life.

Today, sitting in my home in Battle Ground, the quiet feels different. It is not the tense silence of survival, but the gentle peace of restoration. The mask I wore for decades—the one of competence, perfection, and unbreakable strength—is gone. For years, I hid my neurodivergence, treating the unique wiring of my brain as a flaw. I performed and pretended, and it nearly cost me everything. The fire burned that lie away.

Now, the mirror no longer reflects a woman hiding in fear. It shows the truth: the scars, yes, but also a resilience I never knew I possessed. I see a woman who is neurodivergent and whole, a woman who learned that her true self was never something to be ashamed of. I see a woman who is finally free.

This is my resurrection: choosing to live unmasked, to honor my full story, and to trust that the God who sustained me in the darkness is the same

God who now calls me to walk in the light. My story is not one of perfection, but of a persistent, grace-filled rising.

> "You will know the truth, and the truth will set you free."
> —John 8:32 (CSB)

> "The one who started a good work in you will carry it on to completion until the day of Christ Jesus."
> —Philippians 1:6 (CSB)

Reflection: The Courage to Be Seen

There is a moment in every healing journey when pretending becomes heavier than the truth. The mask that once kept you safe begins to choke you. For me, taking it off felt like standing naked in a crowded room—terrifying, vulnerable, and utterly liberating.

Freedom is always found on the other side of honesty. God doesn't bless the version of you that performs; He blesses the one that's real. The one who stumbles over words, needs help, asks for grace, and shows up anyway. The mirror is not your enemy; it's your teacher. It reflects not only what's wounded but also what's still alive, still worthy, and still gloriously becoming.

Affirmation

I no longer hide behind masks. I honor the truth of who God made me to be.

 **Prayer:**

God, thank You for removing the masks I once thought I needed to survive. Thank You for showing me that the truth of who I am is not shameful, but sacred. Help me to live boldly, without apology, trusting that freedom comes from truth. Amen.

Reflection Questions:

1. What masks have you worn to survive, and what has it cost you?
2. How does it feel to look in the mirror and see your true self?
3. What truth do you need to claim about yourself today that will set you free?
4. Where is God inviting you to live more authentically, without fear?

Your Turn: Notes, Affirmation & Personal Prayer

Use this space to write your own reflections.

My Notes:

_____

_____

_____

_____

My Affirmation:

_____

_____

_____

_____

My Prayer:

_____

_____

_____

_____

_____

Bridge: From Mask to Resurrection

When the mask finally fell, I didn't just see myself—I saw the woman God had been resurrecting all along.

The woman beneath the armor wasn't weak; she was weary from pretending. The truth didn't destroy me; it delivered me.

Every layer I peeled away—fear, shame, perfection, performance— revealed a version of me I had buried under the weight of survival. And there, in the stillness, I heard God's whisper: This is who I made you to be.

That realization was my resurrection. Not the loud, triumphant kind you see in movies, but the quiet, holy kind that happens when you choose to live without the armor you once thought kept you safe.

The mask fell. The mirror reflected truth. And from that truth, a new me began to rise.

The Resurrection of Me — Closing Reflection

Resurrection didn't arrive with trumpets. It came quietly—in the mornings I decided to rise, even when nothing felt new. It came through tears that watered the ground of my own rebirth.

This version of me isn't flawless, but she is free. And freedom, I've learned, is not the absence of struggle, but the presence of grace in the middle of it.

What they buried was only the seed. What grew back was purpose.

Testimony Twenty:

A New Pattern

> *"Where I was is not where I am, and where I have been is not where I'm going."*

This is not the story of a woman who never broke. It is the story of a woman who broke and lived; who cried and rose; who carried ashes in her hands and watched God turn them into beauty.

I once prayed for the pain to end and begged God to let me disappear. I once wore masks so heavy they nearly crushed me. But even in those seasons, His hand never let me go. Now, standing on the other side, I can tell you: the same God who carried me will carry you. Your wounds may look different than mine, your storms may come from places my eyes have never seen, but grace is not bound by storylines. Grace will meet you in the fire, in the silence, and in the breaking. It will remind you that survival is not the end—it is the beginning of your resurrection.

The patterns of my past were shaped by trauma, but my present is rich in God's grace because He has been faithful. Every scar I carry is now a testimony. Every crack in my story is a place where His light shines through. And every breath I take is proof that the life trauma tried to bury, God raised back up.

This is my resurrection. And it can be yours, too.

Grace didn't find me when I was polished; it met me when I was undone. It sat beside me in hospital rooms, whispered over sleepless nights, and held me when words failed. I used to think grace was something you earned—something given only to the strong and the unbroken. Now I know it's for the weary, the waiting, the ones still learning how to rise. Grace is the thread that wove my fragments back together, creating a new and beautiful pattern where only brokenness existed before.

I am not where I was, and I am no longer defined by the patterns I learned just to survive. I am living in a new pattern of grace—because I finally let go and allowed God to love and reshape the parts of me I used to hide.

> "My grace is sufficient for you, for my power is perfected in weakness."
> —2 Corinthians 12:9 (CSB)

Reader's Guide

Affirmation

The patterns of my past do not define my future. Grace is my inheritance. I rise, not because I am unbroken, but because God's strength is made perfect in me.

 **Prayer:**

God, thank You for carrying me through fire and silence, through breaking and resurrection. Thank You for showing me a new pattern through Your grace. I offer my life, my story, my scars, and my healing back to You. May they be used for Your glory, and may others see in me the proof that nothing is wasted in Your hands. Amen.

Reflection Questions:

Reflection Questions:
1. Where in your life has God's grace shown up in unexpected ways?
2. How do your scars tell a story of His faithfulness?
3. What is one old pattern you can release today, and what new pattern of grace can you step into?

Your Turn: Notes, Affirmation & Personal Prayer

Use this space to write your own reflections.

My Notes:

_____
_____
_____
_____

My Affirmation:

_____
_____
_____
_____

My Prayer:

_____
_____
_____
_____

Epilogue: Unmasked

"This is what freedom feels like."

For so many years, I thought life was about proving myself—proving I was smart enough, strong enough, worthy enough. I wore masks to survive. I bent myself into shapes that kept other people comfortable. I hid my pain so well that I even started to believe it might not matter.

But standing here now, on the other side of the fire, I know better. Survival was never the end of my story. Resurrection was.

Living unmasked doesn't mean life is perfect. I still flinch sometimes. I still fight old patterns. I still grieve what I lost. But I do it honestly now—with truth on my lips and grace in my heart. I live knowing I am more than the numbers, the labels, the betrayals, or the failures. I am God's child— deeply loved, divinely purposed, and fully free.

And so are you.

> *"Now the Lord is the Spirit, and where the Spirit of the Lord is, there is freedom."*
> *—2 Corinthians 3:17 (CSB)*

God, I thank You for every person holding this book, every heart heavy with stories of survival, every soul longing for resurrection.

Remind them that they are not alone. That their pain is not wasted. That their future is not canceled by their past.

Cover them with Your peace. Strengthen them with Your Spirit. And raise them into the fullness of who You created them to be—unmasked, unafraid, and free.
Amen.

A Benediction

To every reader, no matter your story— May you know that your scars are not the end. May you find the courage to take off the masks you've worn and meet yourself in truth. May you see your reflection not as broken, but as beloved. And may you rise—again and again—into the freedom that was always yours.

Acknowledgments

To God

To God, the Author and Finisher of my faith: You never left me. Not in the shadows, not in the silence, and not in the fire. Every breath I take is because You sustained me. Every word I've written is because You redeemed me. This story is Yours as much as it is mine. Thank You.

To My Family

To my husband, Scott Maniex: Thank you for walking beside me in every season—through fire, faith, and freedom.

To my children—Felisha, Tyler, and Tiana: You are my heart in motion. **And to my 12 grandchildren:** Your joy, love, and laughter are my daily blessings.

To my cousin, sister, and momma in one—Felicia McAllister: You have been my peace for as long as I can remember. Words cannot fully express my love for you, but please know this: I LOVE YOU MORE.

To my little big brother, Robert Winston: I love you. Always.

To my uncles—Raymond Winston, Thomas Winston, and Reed Winston: Thank you for being strong, steady, and positive male figures in my life.

To Momma and Daddy: Thank you for making me, both literally and figuratively.

To my grandmother, Cozzie Mae Winston-Dunlap: You were my rock when I was just a pebble.

To my grandfather, Napolean Winston: You may have been short in stature, but you stood tall in my heart and in my life.

To My Friends & Lifelines

To Alice Williams: Thank you for being someone I can talk to, laugh with, and go to church within truth and realness. You've been a sister to my soul.

To Those Who Heard My Cry

To Laura Keels, NP: Thank you. You saw me when I didn't even realize I needed to be seen. Your intervention changed the course of my healing.

To Dr. Erin Wos: When I first came to you, I was in significant pain and felt that my concerns had not been truly heard elsewhere. Your attentive care and genuine compassion stood out from the very beginning. I was deeply moved by how thoughtfully you addressed my needs—not just as a patient, but as a person and as a Black woman. That level of understanding was exactly what I needed. Your empathy and dedication made all the difference. You truly rock, Doc!

To PeaceHealth ADAPT Plus and Charlie Health: You saved me in 2025. I will be forever grateful for your care, your compassion, and the grace you extended to me when I needed it most.

To My Encouragers

To Michelle Brenk, Stephanie Rosie-Yamashita, Heidi Ross, Klarissa Meinholtz, and Hannah Dario:

The words *thank you* are not sufficient, but they are deeply felt. Thank you for all that you have poured into me over the years. Your presence, encouragement, and unwavering belief have been both anchoring and inspiring. You each hold a place in my story that words can't fully express, but please know: your impact has been eternal.

Epilogue: Unmasked

This is what freedom feels like.

For so many years, I thought life was about proving myself—proving I was smart enough, strong enough, worthy enough. I wore masks to survive. I bent myself into shapes that kept other people comfortable. I hid my pain so well that I even started to believe it might not matter.

But standing here now, on the other side of the fire, I know better. Survival was never the end of my story. Resurrection was.

Living unmasked doesn't mean life is perfect. I still flinch sometimes. I still fight old patterns. I still grieve what I lost. But I do it honestly now—with truth on my lips and grace in my heart.

I live knowing I am more than the numbers, the labels, the betrayals, or the failures. I am God's child—deeply loved, divinely purposed, and fully free.

And so are you.

> "Now the Lord is the Spirit, and where the Spirit of the Lord is, there is freedom."
> —2 Corinthians 3:17 (CSB)

Post-Epilogue: Still Rising
October 3, 2025

Healing is a living thing—it moves, breathes, and evolves with us. Even now, as I write these words, I am still rising. Last night's flashback reminded me that healing isn't linear—it's layered. The scent of body mist and the cool fan breeze brought me back to the night of October 31, 2024—the Vancouver Mall shooting. I could smell it, see it, and feel it unfold like a movie. PTSD is a strange companion—it lingers quietly, like onions, waiting for the right moment to sting. But through therapy, EMDR, and grace, I am learning that each layer peeled back is not just pain—it's progress.

With the holidays approaching, old memories surface—my father's passing in December 1993, his burial on my daughter's birthday, the Christmas of 1986 when I was given a can opener at eleven years old. These moments once made me feel invisible and unwanted, but now they remind me how far I've come. I've learned that the past doesn't disappear—it transforms. Each session of therapy, each breath of prayer, each tear I allow myself to feel is a declaration that trauma will not have the final word.

As I prepare for another surgery—my left wrist and elbow—on October 28, 2025, fear visits me again. But this time, I don't face it alone. I have faith, family, and a Father who never leaves. Healing takes time, and I'm giving myself that time. I'm still rising, still learning, still breathing grace into every scar.

Author's Note of Gratitude

Dear Reader,

Thank you for walking this road with me. Writing these words was not easy—it required me to peel back layers I once thought I would never share. But healing, I've learned, is never meant to stay hidden. It multiplies when it's spoken, when it's witnessed, when it's carried together.

Every chapter you've read is a piece of my story, but I hope you also saw pieces of your own. The faces and names may differ, but the ache of betrayal, the weight of silence, the fire of resilience—these are universal. And so is the hope that rises on the other side.

I pray this book gave you not just my testimony, but also space for your own reflection. That it reminded you that survival is not the end of your story, and that resurrection, however it unfolds in your life—is possible.

Thank you for giving me the honor of sharing this journey with you. My deepest prayer is that you walk away unmasked, unafraid, and free.

With love and gratitude,

Dr. JeVona Maniex

Back Cover Blurb

Hope hides in broken places.

For decades, Dr. JeVona Maniex survived in the silent storm of abuse, betrayal, and unspoken wounds. She built a career and a family, always pushing forward, yet the echoes of trauma remained.

In *Patterned by Trauma*, she doesn't just recount the battles she faced—from childhood neglect to devastating workplace injustice—she reveals the raw, honest path from hidden pain to a resurrected life. With profound spiritual insight, this memoir charts a course from survival to true freedom. It is an invitation to anyone who has ever felt unseen, unworthy, or unsafe to find their own story within these pages and to believe that no wound is too deep for grace to heal.

About the Author

Dr. JeVona Maniex is an organizational psychologist, HR leader, author, speaker, and founder of The Workplace Whisperer: HR & Behavioral Dynamics, LLC. With a PhD in Industrial Organizational Psychology, she combines psychological insight with leadership strategy to help organizations and individuals navigate workplace conflict, resilience, and cultural well-being.

Born in Indiana, Dr. Maniex overcame childhood trauma and the challenges of being a young mother while navigating life as a neurodivergent woman (dyslexia, dysgraphia, and ADHD). Her journey has taught her that survivors don't just endure—they resurrect. Today, she uses her voice to bridge the worlds of faith, leadership, and mental wellness, empowering others to rise from their own ashes.

In addition to her work in Industrial Organizational Psychology, Dr. Maniex is the author of several children's books that inspire courage, self-worth, and emotional awareness in young readers. Through every story she tells—whether written for boardrooms or bedtime—her message remains the same: healing is possible, purpose is powerful, and God's grace transforms everything.

She lives in Washington with her husband and finds joy in faith, family, and the lifelong work of restoration.

Author Website: JeVonaManiex.com

Grace & Grit Books

An Imprint of Dr. JeVona Maniex

Where faith meets fire, and stories rise from the ashes.

Grace & Grit Books is the publishing home for Dr. JeVona Maniex's works of faith, healing, and resilience. From her inspirational memoirs to her uplifting children's stories, each title under this imprint reflects her belief that even in the hardest seasons, grace still restores.

www.ingramcontent.com/pod-product-compliance
Lightning Source LLC
Chambersburg PA
CBHW051636120626
46551CB00014B/2113